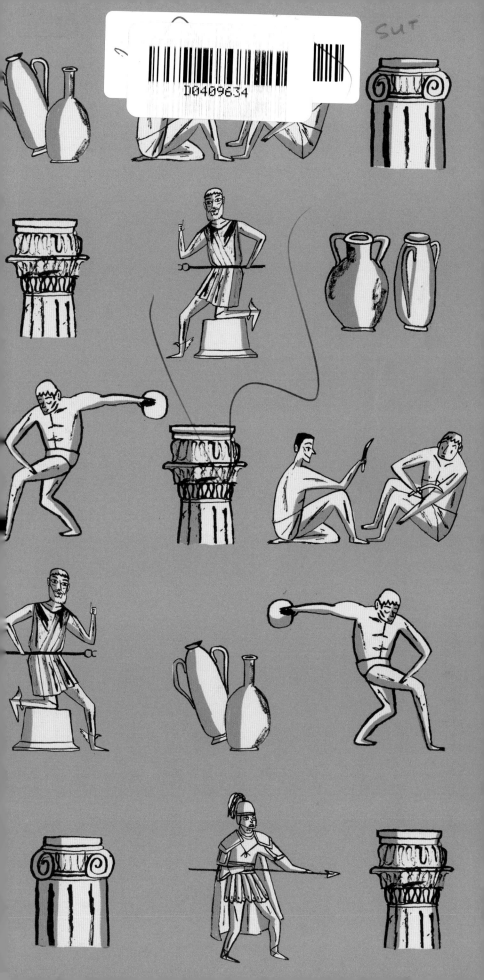

DISCOVER...

THE ROMAN EMPIRE

Illustrated by
Isabel Greenberg

Written by
Imogen Greenberg

Frances Lincoln
Children's Books

Welcome To The Roman Empire

For hundreds of years, stories have been told about the Roman Empire's epic wars and enormous armies, great statesman and treacherous friends. But who were the Romans really?

The Roman Empire began in Italy... in Rome! Rome was founded on the banks of a river called the Tiber, and over time the Romans conquered so much land that it became one of biggest Empires the ancient world ever saw.

As well as conquering people, the Romans were good at other things too, like inventing things! The Romans had central heating — something which wasn't invented in the Western world until almost two thousand years later!

Even though they did some amazing things, what you'll find out in this book is that the Romans were just normal people, like you and me.

We know a lot about how they lived, thanks to historians, who spend their time reading documents to understand more about the Romans, and archaeologists, who uncover Roman artefacts from the past to put together a better idea of how they lived.

In this book you will discover all kinds of secrets about the Romans... and if you're wondering where and when these things happened, turn to the back, where you will find a fold-out map and timeline. Now, come and meet your guides!

KINGS

The Romans were around for hundreds of years. Over time they tried out different ways of ruling. For the first 200 years they had kings. They had a myth about the very first one...

ROMULUS AND REMUS

Numitor was King of Alba Longa until his brother overthrew him and killed all his sons. But his daughter had twin babies, ROMULUS and REMUS by the god Mars. They were left in the river Tiber to die...

But we survived!

A she-wolf found us and suckled us!

... And then a shepherd raised them. Years later, the brothers found out about Numitor and helped restore him to his throne. Then they decided to found a new city together, but argued over where to build it, and Remus was slain. Romulus founded his new city alone, and named it ROME, creating the Senate and the Roman army.

I became the first king...

ROME

And between 753 BC and 509 BC, there were seven kings of Rome altogether!

REPUBLIC 509 BC – 27 BC

In 509 BC, an uprising overthrew the last King of Rome. For the next five hundred years, the SENATE ruled Rome. Each year, they elected two Consuls, who directed the Senate, so no one held power for too long. This was Known as the Roman Republic, and under their rule, the empire grew large.

EMPIRE 27 BC – 476 AD

Eventually, the Republic weakened. The Senate was made up of rich and powerful men, who also ruled the army.

Caesar declared himself Dictator, and the other men murdered him! Civil war broke out and in 27 BC, Augustus won and became the first Roman Emperor. Though the Senate still existed, this was the end of the Roman Republic. Now emperors ruled the ROMAN EMPIRE.

ROMAN
HALL OF

27 BC – 14 AD

AUGUSTUS was Julius Caesar's adopted son. He was only twenty when Caesar was murdered, and not very important. Everyone underestimated him! After Caesar died, there was a civil war, and Augustus won! He made himself the first emperor of Rome.

AUGUSTUS

41 AD – 54 AD

CLAUDIUS was Augustus's great nephew and had little experience of ruling, but he was good at taking advice. He conquered Britain, which many Roman generals had tried to do and failed, and he named his son Britannicus to celebrate.

CLAUDIUS

54 AD – 68 AD

NERO was known as a cruel emperor. In 64 AD there was a huge fire in Rome, and rumours went round that Nero had started it because he wanted to use the land to build himself a palace. They even said he played the fiddle while Rome burnt to the ground!

NERO

RULERS' FAME

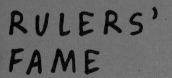

117 AD – 138 AD
HADRIAN is remembered as a great emperor, and was the first to visit every province of his vast empire! Before ruling, he had been a senator and soldier. He famously built the huge Hadrian's Wall between England and Scotland to keep out the Picts.

HADRIAN

306 AD – 337 AD
CONSTANTINE THE GREAT made lots of changes to make the empire stronger. He converted to Christianity, and lots of the Empire did too. He built a new capital to rule from, called Constantinople (which is now called Istanbul).

CONSTANTINE

JUSTINIAN

527 AD – 565 AD
The last great Roman emperor, JUSTINIAN, ruled from Constantinople, when lots of the Empire (including Rome!) had been lost. He tried to get it all back and make the Empire great again. He also brought the many laws of the Empire into one written book.

JULIUS CAESAR

One of the best-known Roman leaders was JULIUS CAESAR (100 BC — 44 BC). He was a powerful general when Rome was a republic.

During his rule, Caesar conquered all of GAUL (now France) and later took BRITAIN too, which was hard to conquer because it was an island and its people were ferocious. He didn't have enough soldiers to hold it.

Julius Caesar fell out with all the other Senators, who were nervous of his power. Caesar was angry that they were ganging up against him, and broke the most important rule in Rome...

Generals weren't allowed in to the city of Rome with their armies, so they couldn't intimidate people into following their orders. Caesar broke the rule when he crossed the river Rubicon, close to the city. The Senators fled, and he declared himself DICTATOR OF ROME.

Caesar was now the most powerful man in the Empire. He went to Egypt to visit the province, and met the beautiful queen CLEOPATRA. They fell in love but couldn't marry, because Caesar already had a Roman wife. Even so, they had a son together called Caesarian. Much later, when the Emperor Augustus invaded Egypt, Cleopatra Killed herself with poison from her pet snaKe.

The Senators were angry about Caesar's power, and didn't want him to destroy the Republic, where they all ruled together. So they plotted to murder him. BRUTUS and CASSIUS led the assassination, which happened at the end of a Senate meeting, in the middle of the floor!

We remember him today because the month of July is named after him!

The Romans were very good at winning battles, and so they started to gain lots of new land, which became the ROMAN EMPIRE. As they got bigger, they made enemies of other great empires.

THE CARTHAGINIANS

Ready to meet the opposition?

First they fought the CARTHAGINIANS, a huge and powerful empire in Africa. There were three great wars between the Roman Republic and Carthage, known as the Punic Wars

The FIRST PUNIC WAR: 264 – 241 BC

This started with a fight over the island of Sicily. The great general HAMILCAR BARCA led the Carthaginians. The Romans destroyed the whole of his fleet, and won.

The SECOND PUNIC WAR: 218 – 201 BC

Hamilcar Barca's son, the general HANNIBAL BARCA, crossed the Alps to invade Italy with an army of 38,000 men, 8,000 horses and 38 elephants!

The freezing Alps were no place for an elephant, and nearly all of them died, but even so, Hannibal was winning! So the Romans attacked Carthage, and Hannibal had to go back to Africa to defend it; the Romans defeated him.

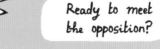

Victory!

The THIRD PUNIC WAR: 146 BC

This time the Romans destroyed the city of Carthage completely.

Bit chilly in the back!

THE PARTHIANS

In the East, the Romans fought the PARTHIANS. Parthia was a ferocious empire in Asia.
In 53 BC, a general named CRASSUS launched a huge attack against them. It was one of the most humiliating defeats the Romans ever faced. They even took the legions' standards — a terrible omen!

THE GOTHS

In the North, the GERMANIC TRIBES lived in the dark forests across the River Rhine. For many years the Romans tried to conquer them but failed.

Haha! Take that Romans!

In 9 AD, the Roman general VARUS was marching his three legions through Teutoburg Forest, when they were ambushed by an allegiance of tribes. They were massacred entirely, making it one of the worst Roman defeats ever.

THE ROMAN ARMY

All this conquering meant the Romans needed a really good army. The army was divided into LEGIONS, each with about 5,000 men.

If your standard was lost or captured, it was a huge disgrace!

Every legion had a STANDARD – a long pole with flags or symbols that showed who they were. The standard of the first legion was a golden eagle, and this was very special.

The soldiers were trained to fight in formation. One formation was called the TORTOISE. The soldiers held their shields up and together to form a barrier that looked like a giant tortoise shell!

You guys okay in there?

We even had to dig our own toilets!

The men could march up to 20 miles in a day. They had to carry tents, food and cooking pots, as well as their weapons and armour. At the end of the day's march, they had to build their CAMP.

When the Romans conquered somewhere, they sent lots of soldiers and appointed new RULERS. They built new cities, which looked like mini Romes, with theatres, games arenas and big public buildings.

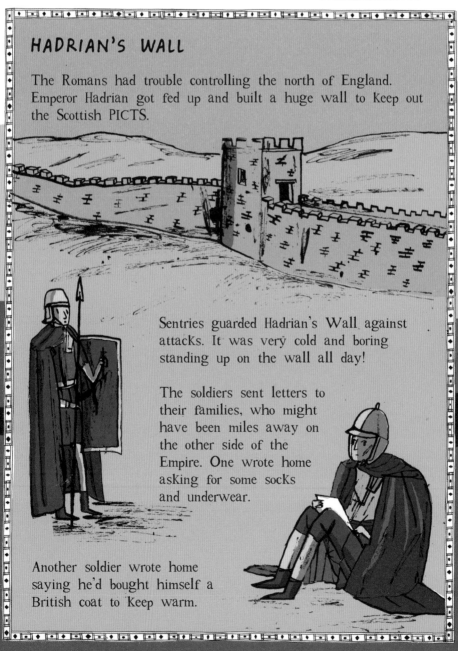

HADRIAN'S WALL

The Romans had trouble controlling the north of England. Emperor Hadrian got fed up and built a huge wall to keep out the Scottish PICTS.

Sentries guarded Hadrian's Wall against attacks. It was very cold and boring standing up on the wall all day!

The soldiers sent letters to their families, who might have been miles away on the other side of the Empire. One wrote home asking for some socks and underwear.

Another soldier wrote home saying he'd bought himself a British coat to keep warm.

... And half was run from Constantinople in the East. There were two emperors and this worked for a while.

CONSTANTINOPLE

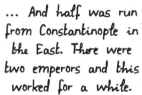

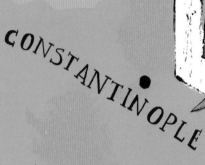

But soon the West got into trouble. Lots of people started to invade, including the Germanic Tribes who crossed the Rhine when it froze in the winter.

The armies couldn't cope and were overrun. In 410 AD, the city of Rome was INVADED and sacked.

The battle for Rome continued for many years. Eventually, in 476 AD, the last Roman Emperor Romulus Augustus was DEPOSED. The Roman Empire in the West ended.

The Empire in the East lasted for hundreds of years after this. They never got Rome back, but still called themselves Romans...

...because Romans are awesome.

The Romans had hundreds of GODS and GODDESSES, which is known as polytheism. Each of them had magical powers – anything you can think of, the Romans could ask a god to help them with it!

Romans told stories, or myths, about their gods, who they believed were all part of a big family. They also thought the gods intervened in their lives — to help them or punish them if they were bad.

When the Empire expanded, the Romans heard about new gods, and what they could do, and sometimes they worshipped them too.

The Romans worshipped in temples, which were built specially for each god, and honoured them in lots of different ways. They PRAYED, left OFFERINGS like wine or food, and sometimes, they SACRIFICED animals. They held huge festivals, where they feasted, drank and sacrificed together.

CHRISTIANITY

After hundreds of years of worshipping many gods, some people, called Christians, started to believe in just one God. This is called monotheism. Christianity thrived under CONSTANTINE THE GREAT.

I have had a divine intervention!

VICTORY will be ours!

But only if we convert to Christianity!

In 312 AD, he had a dream before a battle. It was a sign from God! He won the battle, and so showed his thanks by converting to Christianity and making the entire Roman Empire Christian.

The Romans were around for a long time, and invented lots of things!

You might recognise some of them, because we still use them today.

FAME

SCHOOL

PICTURE

LATIN

Their language was called Latin, and when they invaded somewhere, they took Latin with them. Lots of Latin words are still used, and European languages, like Spanish, Italian and French, have Latin roots.

LAW

Most legal systems in Europe are based on the way the Romans used the law to protect its citizens and make sure they were treated fairly.

However, anybody that came from outside of the Roman Empire had no rights or legal protection at all!

CALENDARS

The Romans invented a calendar with days, weeks and months, similar to the one we use today.

Months were named after important people – July was named after Julius Caesar, August was named after Augustus, and March was named after the god, Mars.

WELFARE

The Romans had many government programmes that helped the people, which even included food for the needy. When grain was expensive, the government helped by giving out cheap grain or sometimes free bread. Augustus was the first emperor to do this.

MEDICINE

The Roman army doctors learned lots of tricks to help save soldiers' lives. They invented clamps so people would lose less blood during surgery, and even invented the Caesarian section to help women give birth.

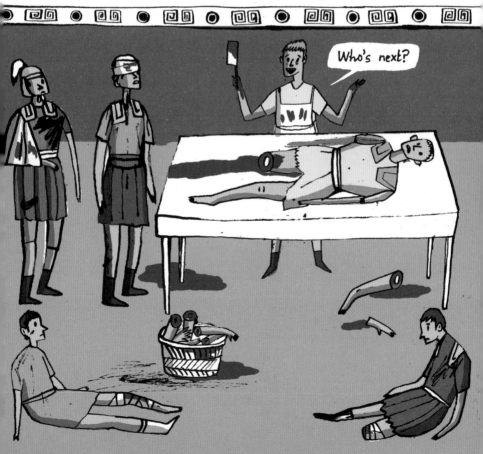

The Romans were amazing at building!

Here are some of the things their builders and engineers created across the Empire.

ROADS

The Romans were the first people to build huge roads to link their empire. That's why people say that 'all roads lead to Rome'!

HEATED HOUSES

The Romans even had central heating! They created raised floors, built on pillars. The space under the floor was filled with hot air from a furnace, which warmed it up!

AQUEDUCTS

The Romans built aqueducts to bring fresh water to towns and cities from far away — long before taps! These aqueducts had huge arches (another Roman invention!).

CONCRETE

The Romans worked out how to set concrete. They were so clever, they could even use it underwater! They also invented reinforced concrete, with supportive metal bars inside.

The Romans decorated their houses with MOSAICS — pictures made from hundreds of tiny pieces of stone.

Roman cities needed aqueducts, roads and sewers, as well as the fun stuff like baths, temples, arenas, shops and libraries. Together, they made a large and bustling Roman city!

Rich Romans had luxurious lives. They lived in stone houses, with lots of rooms. They were built around a little courtyard, called an ATRIUM, where they had other rich Romans round for dinner. Feasts could be very elaborate, to show off to their friends.

Rich Roman men wore TOGAS, a huge piece of fabric draped over one shoulder and around their body. Senators had special togas, so everyone knew they were important.

Rich Roman women wore a long dress called a STOLA... like this!

So fancy!

Rich households also had SLAVES. These people were the property of the household, and so they worked for them but were not paid.

Poorer Romans could live in the city, in wooden houses. Or they could live in the countryside in modest houses on small farms.

The clothes for us poorer folk were woven from cheaper cloth. The men wore TUNICS and the women wore cheaper dresses. They would have very little jewellery or valuables.

The most common food was porridge and bread, often from the CORN DOLE — grain given out by the government. No stuffed partridge for us!

Romans weren't just 'rich' or 'poor' though. Lots of people led comfortable lives as soldiers, traders, blacksmiths or craftsmen.

Some entrepreneurial Romans travelled the whole Empire to make some more money.

ROMAN RELAXATION

Romans didn't always have water in their own houses, so they went to big communal BATH HOUSES. They got together there and chatted, or even met people who they worked with to discuss business.

First of all, baths were divided into men and women.

The men started off by lifting weights, wrestling or swimming — just like a gym.

Then they'd scrape the dirt and oil off their bodies
with a tool called a STRIGIL.

Good hustle out there today.

Thanks dude.

Then they'd go to the bath house.
Baths were divided into men and women.
They started in the TEPIDARIUM,
a warm room, a bit like a sauna.

Then they moved to
the CALDARIUM –
a very hot pool of
water, like a jacuzzi.

Brrrrrrr.

Then
they finished in
the FRIGIDARIUM,
a very cold room!

Some baths were really
big, with gardens, a cafe
and even a library. People could
spend the whole day there!

The most famous amphitheatre, the COLOSSEUM in Rome, took nearly ten years to build! We guess that between 50,000 and 80,000 Romans could fit in there to watch the games and gladiator fights.

On special occasions, there could be days and days of fights for the city's entertainment, often in honour of the imperial family – and paid for by them, too! At the end of a fight, when one gladiator had the other at his mercy, he would look to the emperor (or another VIP), and wait for his signal to kill or spare his opponent.

DAILY LIFE OF A GLADIATOR

Gladiators were usually SLAVES who were trained to fight for sport and entertainment. Sometimes, they fought chained tigers. Other times, they fought on chariots with horses. Many gladiators died fighting, but the best ones could become rich and famous, and even win their freedom.

In 79 AD, a huge volcano erupted in southern Italy. The ash from the volcano buried an entire Roman city, called POMPEII. Lots of people died and it was a great tragedy.

Hundreds of years later, ARCHAEOLOGISTS started to dig up this forgotten city. They found huge mansions, shops, baths, theatres, stadiums, streets and houses.

We've even found loaves of bread that had been baking when the volcano erupted.

When archaeologists find things, they are called ARTEFACTS. We ask questions like "What is it?" "Who might have used it?", "Where did it come from?", "What is it called?" and "What does it do?"

It is hard to tell an artefact's story from just one object, so we compare it with other objects, and examples of when it was mentioned in books or pictures. Here is one of my favourite artefacts...

These are AMPHORAE. The Romans used them to carry goods like olive oil. They were large and not very practical to move around, but they were useful for trading because they could hold so much inside. Hundreds were loaded onto ships to be sold across the Empire. We know this because marine archaeologists have found Roman shipwrecks full of amphorae, ready to be traded!

ISABEL GREENBERG is a London-based comic
artist, illustrator and writer. She enjoys
illustrating all things historical.

IMOGEN GREENBERG is a London-based writer,
who loves to write about history, and is editor
of The Story Finders.

Discover... The Roman Empire copyright © Frances Lincoln Ltd 2016
Text copyright © Imogen Greenberg 2016
Illustrations copyright © Isabel Greenberg 2016

The right of Imogen Greenberg to be identified as the author
and Isabel Greenberg to be identified as the illustrator of this work
has been asserted by them in accordance with the Copyright,
Designs and Patents Act, 1988 (United Kingdom).

First published in Great Britain in 2016 by Frances Lincoln Children's Books,
74-77 White Lion Street, London N1 9PF
QuartoKnows.com
Visit our blogs at QuartoKnows.com

A catalogue record for this book is available from the British Library.

ISBN 978-1-84780-826-4
Illustrated digitally
Designed by Nicola Price • Edited by Jenny Broom

Printed in China
1 3 5 7 9 8 6 4 2

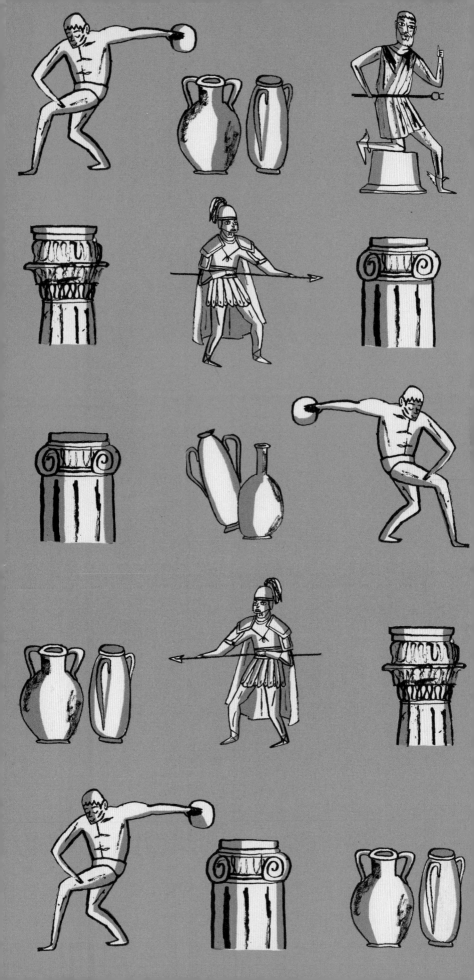